LIFTING THE LID

on Stress, Anxiety and Depression

by

Chris Scott

Illustrations by
Tomas Woodbridge

By the same author

Goodbye to God: Searching
for a *Human* Spirituality

ISBN – 978-1-911076-17-9

To
Ruth, Freya and Tian

Acknowledgements

My thanks go to Tom Woodbridge for his great illustrations that bring the text to life.

To my wife Ruth, especially for her encouragement in keeping me at the writing process. Also to my friends Sue Sabbagh, John Lilley and Anna Ford for checking over my script with their astute sense for good grammar and correct form.

Thanks also go to Joe Griffin and Ivan Tyrrell, the co-founders of the Human Givens Institute. By synthesising the results of their own research, the best current practice in psychotherapy and the latest discoveries from neuro-science, they have created a methodology that is highly effective in treating stress, anxiety and depression.

Foreword

In spite of overwhelming evidence relating the increasing frequency of depression to social and work stresses, and particular thinking styles, depression is often talked about as a disease that strikes without rhyme or reason, and for which the remedy is to "correct the chemical imbalance". This is rather like seeing obesity as a "disease" which needs "treatment" by a specialist. Whilst this is certainly true in some cases, it does not apply to the vast majority.

In both cases the remedy lies, in large part, in explaining the paths that lead to the entrapment and the steps that need to be taken to break free. Chris Scott has done this admirably for people suffering from stress, anxiety and depression in this short and lucid book.

Farouk Okhai
MBCHB, MRC Psych
Consultant Psychiatrist
Milton Keynes Primary Care Trust

Introduction

Depression is one of the fastest growing diseases in the world. Thousands more people are suffering from it than ever before, and sufferers are getting younger and younger; and hardly a conversation will be had without the word "stress" cropping up some-where.

There are countless books on the market explaining stress, anxiety and depression. Some suggest methods of overcoming them. One or two are excellent, but mostly they are full of theory and psychobabble, difficult to read and even harder to understand. Some are, not to put too fine a point on it, total rubbish. They take theories stemming from a nineteenth century understanding of psychology, and weave mind-boggling concepts that serve only to build mystery around the subject.

"The boy develops an object carthexis for his mother and jealousy and hostilty towards his father. He develops a fear of castration, whilst the girl thinks she has already been castrated".
- Freud

What we have ended up with is cult-like schools of psychotherapy where the expectation is that the unfortunate sufferer will spend years in therapy that will cost them an arm and a leg.

But, thank goodness, a combination of both up-to-the-minute psychological research and brain science has shown what depression really is, and how to deal with it quickly and efficiently.

It needs to be said here that mental health runs along a continuum. Mental ill health is not something that 'just happens'. It creeps up on us. It could be seen to be a bit like this:

Fine and dandy → acute stress (ok) → chronic stress (not ok) → depression → acute anxiety & panic attacks → breakdown → hallucinations → barking mad

Fine and dandy – A person's needs are being met in a balanced way by their own set of innate resources and by their environment.

Acute stress – This comes from the pressures of life that happen to us occasionally. Some intermittent pressure can actually help stimulate people into greater action.

Chronic stress – Not so good. This is where the pressures of life keep piling up without resolution, our needs are unmet and/or our resources are either insufficient for the tasks, or not being used enough for life to be satisfying.

Depression – The body/mind balance starts to go askew and our energy supply is drained from us.

Acute anxiety and panic attacks - The body starts acting as though it's in a war zone because our stress hormones have become all out of kilter.

Breakdown – The body/mind balance gets so out of balance that we just come to a grinding halt, mentally and/or physically.

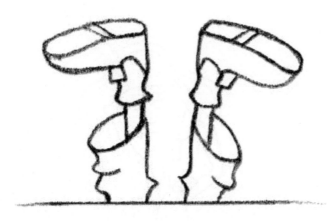

Hallucinations (very rare) – The world of dream sleep starts to break into our waking times and we begin to think that the images or voices from our dreams are really out there in the world.

Barking mad (very, very rare) – A complete breakdown between the 'real' world and that of hallucinations. All sense of 'reality' is lost.

The thing to do is to stop it *before* it progresses too far.

(It should be noted that relatively few people get as far as breakdown, and only a very tiny minority beyond that point.)

Some of the symptoms of chronic stress and depression are:

- Low mood
- Disturbed sleep patterns
- Change of appetite
- Digestive problems (ranging from indigestion to irritable bowel and stomach ulcers)
- Aches and pains
- Tiredness
- Feeling exhausted when you wake (your get up and go has got up and gone)
- Little or no motivation, even for things you used to enjoy.

This is a short guide and it will not go into great depth or detail. What you will find between these covers is a simple explanation of what causes stress, anxiety and depression, and ways to help yourself, friends or family recover quickly from its grip. When using the simple guidelines in this book, many people will almost certainly gain rapid relief from their symptoms and start to enjoy life again.

Towards the end of this book you will find five things you can do to help reverse the effect of chronic stress anxiety and depression. Start doing them today, and begin to feel the difference by tomorrow!

(But read the bits in between as well, or you won't get the five points!)

Stress and depression have causes, they don't just happen for no reason. As human beings we, like every other living thing, have certain needs that have to be met in a balanced way if we are to be healthy. A simple house-plant has needs, but give it sufficient water, sunlight and a drop of Baby Bio now and again and it will thrive. But we, in our vastly greater complexity, have multiple physical and psychological needs which also have to be satisfied if we are to thrive. We also have a lot of natural resources to help us get those needs met. Above the basic need for food and shelter – the survival needs – there are other needs which are the givens of our human nature. These are:

The need for autonomy and control. Everyone needs to feel that they have a degree of control over the way their life goes. This can be seen very early on as infants begin to express their self-will.

The need for attention. People have very different levels of attention need, but nobody wants to be ignored or treated as if they don't matter.

The need to be emotionally connected. We are social animals and need, in differing degrees, to have emotionally fulfilling relationships with others.

The need to be valued. There is a need to feel of value to others. Again, look at small children, how often they say "look at me, look at *me*!" They want to feel that they matter to someone, especially their mum and dad.

The need for meaning and purpose. The human brain needs to be stretched so that there is a sense of satisfaction. Being under stretched and bored (teachers take note!) can cause as much stress as being over-stretched.

Aesthetic needs. We know that people can survive in awful conditions, but human beings need to be able to feel that "there's more to life than this". We need food for our 'soul'.

A need for privacy and personal space. To differing degrees, people need a certain level of personal space. If this space is chronically violated, stress will follow.

These are some of our basic human givens, and when they are not met, we get sick!

* It should be noted here, that when I use the words 'chronic' or 'chronically', I mean constant and long-lasting. I am not referring to the severity, which may range from mild to severe.

Chapter 1

Where it all began.

Go back in your imagination a few hundred thousand years. Humankind was evolving on the African plains. The most important thing was survival. There was no 'keeping up with the Flintstones', "Well, just look at her new sabre- tooth tiger coat, I must have one of those". Just staying alive was a total occupation.

Early man.

Our brain has evolved to make this a priority. Staying alive, as an individual and as a species, was all that mattered – safety, food, shelter, sex – not much time for anything else. For most of our history, hundreds of thousands of years, this has been the case. Only in very recent time, the last three or four thousand years, have things been less basic. In human history, we are talking about the last few seconds of the last minute of the last hour of the human 'day'.

So survival is high on the agenda of the evolving brain. For most of our history we have been a nice tasty snack for wild beasts, or even other humans. Right in the middle of our brain there is a 'guard'. It is there to protect us. It is a fantastic little thing. It remembers everything from our personal history, and some instinctive stuff as well. It's checking for threats to safety, food sources, sexual partners – in fact anything that requires action for survival. As soon as it recognises something out there in the real world, it sounds the alarm and sends stress hormones into our body. We are ready to fight, freeze or run like hell, have sex, or engage in some other life preserving activity. The heart starts beating faster, we breathe more quickly, the muscles get filled with blood – it's *action stations*.

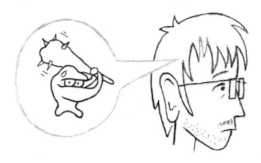

The guard.

Now this bit of the brain has done a fantastic job. Well, as a species we are still around aren't we? But there is a down side. It can't tell the difference between a real threat, (hungry lion) things we are just getting stressed about, or our own worries or imagination. Example: You're in the cinema watching a film, when suddenly an alien leaps out of somebody's stomach. Now unless you've seen the clip before and know what to expect, the chances are your heart will race, your palms will go sweaty and your breathing rate will increase – you're ready for action. The guard in your brain (it's called the amygdala by the way) has sent out the message to release stress hormones *before* your thinking brain (the neo-cortex) has even had time to process the information. As soon as it does, it can reassure the guard that it's only a film, and it can stand down the stress hormones.

Now here's the rub. In earlier times, when the guard sent out the stress hormones, they were needed. There was a hungry lion or a marauding warrior, so we really needed those hormones to prepare us for flight or flight. We either fought, ran or died. As a result, the stress hormones were then used up by fighting or running, or both, and balance returned to the body-brain system.

Life was simpler then.

Unfortunately this is no longer the case. When our guard sends out the stress hormones these days it is, on the whole, very unlikely to be because we are physically under threat and need to fight or run away. The things that 'threaten' us today are much more likely to be psychological dangers than physical ones. At the end of a day full of worries and concerns, our guard has been pumping stress hormones into our body like there is no tomorrow, but it's got nowhere to go. There's nowhere to run and no fighting to do. Physically we are all charged-up, but there is nothing to do with it. We are ready to go into emotional overload. (The guard is part of the emotional brain [the limbic system] and emotion is to do with movement and energy. It is much more instinctive and primitive than the thinking brain. Remember, it's about survival – food, sex, safety etc.) This emotional overload – the chronic secretion of stress hormones with no way of using them up – is what we call "being stressed".

Chapter 2

Understanding Stress

It's really important that we understand what being stressed actually is, so let's try and break it down a bit, because it can get rather confusing. The word stress is used in different ways by different people, so we'll start by defining it for use in this book. Stress can be described as the pressure put upon human beings. It can be mental, physical or psychological pressure. It might be pressure coming upon us from the outside, or pressures we place upon ourselves. It is usually pressure to act in a particular way, complete a task or goal, or to achieve a particular end. The stress mechanism in itself is a physical reaction which is built into our make-up as human beings. As we saw in the last chapter, it is an auto-response system which is activated within us when action of some kind is needed to protect or preserve us. As such it can be said that the stress mechanism is good, because it does a protective or enabling job. But because modern life is *so* different from the way we have lived for most of human history, the stress mechanism can be activated inappropriately, and that is bad, I mean *really* bad. So the definition I will use in this book is:

Stress: That which *inappropriately* activates the flight or fight response in human beings and may cause deterioration in mental, physical or psychological wellbeing.

Let me try and put this in plain words by way of a couple of analogies. The first is for those among you who are 'petrol heads', or, if not as keen as Lewis Hamilton or Chris Evans, you like your cars.

Many cars today are turbo-charged. They have that extra gizmo under the bonnet which, when you put your foot down on the accelerator, squirts fuel mixture into the engine at an increased rate to give you an extra boost. This is well and good, albeit expensive on the pocket if you use it too much. You need to overtake? Give it some wellie, the turbo-charger cuts in, the engine roars and away you go, safely past Doris or Dan who is driving at precisely

22.5 mph on a narrow, bendy country road with few opportunities to pass.

But what would happen if, instead of using the turbo-charger for occasional bursts of speed when we need it, we used it all of the time? What if we stayed in second gear all the way from London to Birmingham with our foot on the floor, with the turbo-charger pumping fuel like there's no tomorrow, and the rev counter permanently in the red? At the very least, we would run out of fuel very quickly and come to a standstill. But more likely, we would do some very expensive damage to our engine, and the car would be off the road for some time.

The body's stress reaction is like the turbo-charger. It squirts hormones into the body for that instant burst of energy, it's our overtaking mechanism, but it is not designed for constant (chronic) use. If the stress response is used chronically, one of two things will happen: Either we will operate at full pelt for a period and then just run out of fuel, or we will damage the engine (mind-body system) and become ill. People who worry or ruminate a lot have the worst of both worlds. The worry or rumination kicks off the stress response (turbo-charger), but they are not actually *doing* anything with all that extra energy, it's like pushing the accelerator and the brake at the same time!

Modern turbo-charged cars are a wonder of mechanical and electrical engineering, but even the best would not perform well, or even survive, if chronically misused. Our bodies are the same, except that they are infinitely more complex and wonderful than anything yet made by humans. Chronic stress *will* lead to ill health because our bodies have evolved the stress mechanism *for acute use only.*

The second analogy is one almost everyone can relate to, the taking of stimulants. Most people drink tea, coffee, or soft drinks like Coke. Some people smoke and/or drink alcohol, and there are numerous other substances, both legal and illegal that people take to give themselves a boost. Most people do it in moderation, in small amounts, and it helps them get through the day. But those people who take too much, either in strength or quantity, end up feeling less good for the experience. Too much strong coffee can give you the jitters, too much alcohol can leave you feeling – well, most of us knows what *that* feels like, and too much sugar or carbohydrate goes straight to the waistline after it's given the brain a bit of a zing on the way. I know a couple of teenagers who decided to drink loads of Red Bull all in one go. They ended up almost running across the ceiling and it took them quite some time to come down from their high. At the far end of the spectrum, there are people who finish up in rehab, or on the streets, because what can be helpful as an acute boost has become a destructive chronic habit.

The body's stress mechanism is our natural reaction to acute emergency or action situations, and as such it is very good. But when it is fired–

off chronically, all day and every day, it becomes as destructive as overdosing with stimulants, or revving your car engine to oblivion.

Now to some degree, most of us get overloaded with stress hormones during the course of the day, for there are always situations that activate the stress system, but which we can't deal with there and then. When we go to bed at night, the stress reactions (feelings/emotions) are still 'alive' in our autonomic nervous system (the bit we have no conscious control over). Fortunately, nature has provided ways of dealing with emotional overload. It has a very neat system that uses our own memories to act out the emotions for us. It's called dreaming.

Chapter 3

Dream on Kid

Dreaming has mystified us for as long as we've known about it, - probably before recorded history. Greek philosophers speculated about it, religions thought it was the voice of God or angels, and psychology since the nineteenth century has come up with more theories about it than most of us have had hot dinners. Freud and Jung are probably the best known amongst modern dream interpreters. For the most part, the majority of people thought that their theories were somewhat off the wall (many courses in academic psychology would hardly mention them, if at all). But their followers clung to these ideas as if received 'from above'. Even today, some continue to follow these Masters with cult-like devotion. I must admit to having been one such myself, thinking at one point that Jung's theories were unarguably correct).

Sigmund Freud

That is not to say that they did not do some ground-breaking work - they certainly did. But it was of their time, and they were men of their time, and we have moved on. In all things we keep pace with advances in science and understanding, and therapeutic psychology isn't exempt from this rule.

Carl Gustav Jung

And as our knowledge widens we must let the past go, not preserve it as inflexible dogma. Jung was a scientist as well as a mystic, I am sure that if he had lived to see the advance of modern neuroscience, he would have modified his views accordingly.

And while, today, at the margins, we're still wading through a mire of theories about dreaming, more recent research really does lift the lid on the purpose of dreams. Combining both physical brain research and psychological research, one author, Joe Griffin seems to have really cracked what dreaming does for us. If you're interested, he and his co-author, Ivan Tyrrell, present a full account in their book, 'Why We Dream'. But in this brief text I'll

45

try to keep it short and simple.

At the end of each day dreaming is nature's way of ridding us of all the emotional arousal we've built up. Every day our guard pumps out stress hormones to help us deal with a range of problems: "You're hungry, go and eat", "You fancy that guy or girl, go and have sex". "Your manager has just bawled you out, punch him on the nose". And so on.

If the guard assesses that there is a really big threat (your exam finals, for instance, or your driving test) it sends out a flood of stress hormones. It wants you to act *now,* so shuts off the thinking brain. This might seem a strange thing to do, but don't forget, it wants immediate *action.* Standing around thinking "I wonder if this sabre tooth tiger is hungry?" is not a good idea.

What the guard tells you to do.

Unfortunately, in modern society, an immediate response can be a distinct disadvantage (when taking your exams for instance). It's also a bad idea when we are driving. Road rage is a great example of what happens when a person gets overtaken by his or her own hormones. The fight part of the 'fight or flight' response cuts in, and motorists become little more than animals at the wheel, totally under the influence of their own stress hormones. It's true to say that raised emotion (whatever the emotion may be) reduces us to stupidity. The more emotional we become, the less access we have to our thinking brain. (Remember, the only thing the guard wants us to do is act, – the consequences are incidental).

But in modern society, of course, acting first and thinking later is rarely appropriate. Mixed-sex work places would become intolerable. People would either be having sex all over the place, or feel grossly harassed, if we let our emotional brains call the shots. Rather, we rely on our thinking brain to soften the guard's instincts: "Not now, this is not appropriate if you want to keep your job and marriage intact". In short, we get on with life in a civilised manner.

But at the end of each day, all those emotional promptings we didn't act on are still churning in our system, and if this were to happen day after day without being discharged, we would simply become overloaded, and mentally and physically exhausted extremely rapidly.

Enter the dreams. To discharge the emotional arousals of the previous day *that we have not been able to act out,* our brain calls upon memories stored away from our earliest days up to the present moment. It uses these stored memories to discharge the arousal, leaving us with a 'clean slate' for the next day. It's a very efficient system, what Joe Griffin calls the "emotional flush toilet".

"So", you might ask, "why are my dreams so weird?" Well it's because the dream uses our stored memories metaphorically. The things we experience in our dreams *represent* the emotionally arousing events of the previous day. People and things we experience in our dreams are never (with a very few exceptions) themselves. They are symbolic matches that are near enough to do the job of cancelling out the arousal. But remember, this only applies to the events *we were not able to act out.*

Example: During the day, my boss is unreasonable and heavy-handed with me, but I don't feel able to speak up for myself. In my dream, a teacher I had at school, who was also heavy-handed, is getting roundly ticked off by my big brother. The teacher is a metaphor for my boss, and my big brother is that part of myself that wants to 'be a man'. The teacher who represents 'heavy-handedness' could appear in any number of dreams, and will be a metaphor for that type of person or behaviour.

For most of us, most of the time, by the end of a normal night's sleep we have had about 25% dream sleep, and this has wiped the slate clean ready for another day.

So what goes wrong?

Chapter 4

Modern society

The problem is that our physical evolution has not caught up with our modern ways of living. As we have seen, the guard is all about protection of the species. For hundreds of thousands of years when it told us to act, it was because we needed to act. As a result, there weren't huge amounts of emotional arousal left undischarged at the end of each day. If we were still alive, we had been acting out such arousals as and when necessary, and clearing the system for another day.

Not so today. In modern society there are a thousand and one things that will set the guard off, but often without the smallest possibility that those emotional arousals will be acted on. In turn, this leaves greater amounts of stress hormones in the body with no place to go.

(It is interesting to note that in communities like the Amish People of North America, who live a simple lifestyle where all their basic needs are fulfilled on a daily basis, clinical depression is virtually unknown.)

At the end of each day, the stresses and strains, worries and ruminations will all have been alerting the guard that something is wrong, or that action of some kind is required. (And remember, it can't tell the difference between a real physical threat and just a bad hair day).

The result of this, is that we have to have a lot more dream sleep to wipe the slate clean for the following day.

"What's wrong with that?" you may ask? Plenty. As we have seen already, 'normal' sleep consists of about 25% dream sleep, the rest is slow wave sleep. During this remaining 75% of sleeping time, our body gets repaired and refreshed, and glucose reserves in the brain get replenished.

All this enables us to wake up in the morning bright eyed and bushy tailed and ready for the next day's work or play.

Not only does too much dream sleep push out the necessary slow wave sleep, but it uses up more energy in the process. Dream sleep is a highly active state that actually uses up more energy than when we are awake. Something called the 'orientation response' that keeps us alert and on the look-out for possible dangers during the day, is firing off during dream sleep. Imagine a photographic flash-gun constantly firing off, it wouldn't take long before the batteries run down. Just so with us.

The highly active state of dream sleep uses

up energy, so if we are having to dream a lot to counteract the emotional arousals of the previous day, we can get to the point where we are using up more energy at night than is being replaced. People who are highly stressed experience far too much dream sleep, and insufficient slow wave sleep. The result is disturbed sleep patterns and waking up in the morning feeling as though you have run a marathon. Sound familiar?

Of course, when we wake up feeling like yesterday's cold porridge, with no energy or enthusiasm, it is even harder to improve matters. The consequence of this is more worry and rumination that alerts the guard to danger, so re-starting the cycle of sending out ever more stress hormones that also have 'nothing to do and no place to go'. This results in – you've guessed it – too much dream sleep – which results in waking up feeling exhausted. And so on.

Depression then can be no more mysterious than this: It is a cycle of excessive emotional arousal and stress hormones caused by a guard that is still tuned into a world of sabre tooth tigers. This leads to too much dream sleep, which leads to feeling like death warmed up when we wake in the morning. It's a twenty four hour cycle that feeds on itself. If circumstances change, it can lift like the morning mist. If we get deeply into it, it can last for months, years or even decades. And into this picture can creep the dreaded twin to depression – anxiety.

Chapter 5

Anxiety

As we have seen in the introduction, stress, depression and anxiety are all part of a continuum, and people are affected in different ways. I think we can look at it like this:

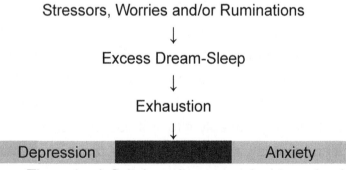

Stressors, Worries and/or Ruminations
↓
Excess Dream-Sleep
↓
Exhaustion
↓

Depression | Anxiety

There is definitely a large overlapping chunk between depression and anxiety, and it would very difficult, not to say downright daft, to try and make a clear distinction between these two emotional states. Both are reactions to either stressful events in our lives, or our tendency to worry or ruminate too much, or a combination of the two.

General anxiety is the feeling of dread which is there first thing on waking in the morning, and which hovers around all day just waiting for the opportunity to give you the jitters. It's there when you put your head on the pillow at night, and when you wake at 3.00am. And it's there when you have to do that routine task that you've probably done a thousand times before, but which now feels like being asked to do a high-wire routine without a net or safety harness.

So what is this little devil that makes life so difficult? Put simply, it's the fear or action response in us that has become over sensitive and cannot switch off. For some reason, the guard has forgotten how to go into standby mode, and constantly thinks there is some sort of danger to be aware of. Whatever the original event, or chain of events, that caused this over sensitivity in our guard, it or they may not be consciously remembered by us. It may have been a single traumatic event in the near or distant past, or it might be due to chronic long-term distress like bullying, or some form of abuse or harassment. Or it might just be that we have been trying to squeeze a quart (almost a litre for younger readers) into a pint pot for far too long and our body has forgotten how to relax.

For many people reading this book and following the advice given in later chapters will be enough to diminish and relieve their symptoms of anxiety. Others may need to make a very conscious effort to do extra things that are relaxing and stress releasing. Using a stress busting CD on a regular basis might be helpful, or treating yourself to a massage, or a session of shiatsu. Spending time with your feet up with a glass of something nice is a good idea, or taking time to enjoy relaxed sex with your partner may be the thing. Perhaps saying "sod it" to the ironing and spending an extra half-hour in the park with the dog would do it.

Now, If you're saying to yourself "I haven't got time for all that!" it's probably a good indication that you've got the balance wrong somewhere in your life, and the anxiety that you are experiencing is your body's way of saying to you "calm down". Or, to use the analogy from chapter two, it's saying; "I'm being over-revved, for God's sake take your foot off the accelerator!"

For some people, one reaction that the body may have is that of a panic attack. This is a very frightening occurrence for the sufferer, in which they might experience some of the following symptoms:

1. Pounding heart
2. Sweating
3. Trembling or shaking
4. A feeling of being smothered or shortness of breath
5. Chest pain or discomfort
6. Feeling sick
7. Feeling faint or dizzy
8. Feeling 'out of it' as if you are not quite all there.
9. A fear of losing control or going crazy.
10. Fear of dying
11. Tingling or a feeling of numbness.

A panic attack is set off by the guard. For some reason it gets it into it's head that there is something really frightening around, although at a conscious level, we may not be aware of it at all. It sends out the *all systems go!* signal, which fills the body with action hormones. So we end up with a body that's got a full head of steam and raring to go, but at a conscious level, we don't know what the hell's going on, or why we feel this way. For those of you who have never experienced a panic attack, just imagine that you have got yourself all geared-up for an important event. It might be a vital sports competition, an examination or a driving test. You are all keyed-up and ready to go when – it's cancelled. Can you imagine how you would feel? For a while you just wouldn't know what to do with yourself. All that built-up tension and nothing to do with it! Now multiply that by a factor of about twenty, and you'll have some idea how a panic attack feels. Assuming the person is in good health in every other way, vigorous exercise can help ease the sensations of a panic attack. Exercise works by using up the hormones that have been released for just that purpose – action, and brings the body back into balance again

For some people, using the techniques in this book may not be enough *in themselves* to alleviate the causes and symptoms of anxiety. If this is the case, they would benefit from a few sessions with an appropriately trained counsellor or therapist. Sometimes anxiety can lead to very specific problems and symptoms like Phobias (irrational fears), Post Traumatic Stress Disorder (PTSD) or Obsessive-Compulsive Disorder (OCD). All of these conditions generally respond well to the sort of solution-focused therapy practiced by Human Givens counsellors and therapists amongst others.

(To find a Human Givens Therapist, there is a web-site reference at the back of the book, and a more general counselling website. Or ask your GP. Many doctors are now referring patients to counsellors and Human Givens practitioners).

Chapter 6

Changing the pattern

The twenty four hour cycle of depression, with or without symptoms of anxiety, is caused by our guard sending out too many stress hormones, which then affects our dream sleep pattern. But why is it that some people seem to get stressed, depressed or anxious more easily than others? Well it's partly to do with our thinking styles. Remember, the guard does not need external events to set it off: Our own imagination will do fine on its own.

A good imagination is all that is required. For instance, it's true to say that young men can get an erection just by looking at two iced cup cakes with cherries on top.

Our thinking style will greatly affect whether or not we will be prone to depression. Example:

Fred goes into work and gets an earful from his manager. His response is; "Silly old sod must have got out of bed the wrong side this morning". Jim gets the same earful, but thinks; "Oh dear, have I done something to upset him? Perhaps he's unhappy with my work. Maybe I'll get the sack and I won't be able to pay the mortgage. The wife and the kids and I will all end up homeless!" No prizes for guessing which of these two guys is more likely to suffer from depression.

Our imagination is a very powerful tool. Humankind is where it is today for better and for worse, thanks to its memory and imagination because we can learn from the past and visualise the future. All the wonderful achievements of humankind were originally conjured up in the imagination; but so too were the death camps of Auschwitz and Bergen-Belsen.

All great sports people and athletes not only practice for real, they do it in their mind as well. They visualise that winning shot, or leap or run. They know that what we visualise in our mind, our brain tries to complete in the outside world. Look at a rugby player getting ready to take that penalty shot. It's quite clear that he (or occasionally she) is visualising the ball going between the posts. They are rehearsing in their imagination what they want to happen in reality. If we're expecting the worst, it is much more likely to happen, not least because by using our imaginations negatively we'll be priming our guard to start emitting stress hormones. If we go through life like Winnie the Pooh's friend Eeyore, constantly expecting the worst, then we won't be disappointed with the results!

In fact, the very wiring of our brain is partially a product of how we think and act. Habits that we form – our ways of thinking and physical habits – are locked into our neural wiring. Habits are things we have practised often enough to become second nature. We no longer have to think of them consciously. And changing our habits of thought or action simply calls for effort, determination and practice.

One of the major causes of anxiety and depression, and that which keeps people anxious or depressed, is worrying and ruminating. Remember, our guard can't tell the difference between a real threat and our own worrying thoughts. Once we have cottoned-on to the fact that our thinking style can push us into anxiety and depression, and keep us there, we need to act on that knowledge.

It's time to stop sitting on our butts and *do* something instead.

Chapter 7

Time for Action

This is not a magic cure.
You have got to help yourself.
Take action, don't just read about it!

Action One – Act on your knowledge

Realise what is going on. Knowing that your anxiety or depression is no more or less than your stress hormones getting the upper hand, gives you control once more. With knowledge comes choice. Knowing what is causing your anxiety or depression lets you refuse to be a victim of it.

You can now choose to act and think differently. *I'm not saying that this is easy.* Learning to play a musical instrument or drive a car is not easy. What is required is commitment and practice and practice and practice. Changing your thinking style and attitude takes just as much dedication, perhaps more.

Action Two – Tell the worry to "Bugger off"

This is the single most important thing you can do to help yourself. Stop worrying. Easier said than done, I know, but it is the door through which you must pass to defeat your anxiety or depression. Remember, your guard is filling you with stress hormones whenever you worry or ruminate on things you cannot do anything about.

So here's the plan. *Every time* you catch yourself worrying or ruminating, ask yourself this: "What can I *do* about it *right now*?" And 99 times out of a 100 the answer will be: nothing. That being the case – and not forgetting the effect of worry on the guard – dismiss the thought in no uncertain terms. 'Bugger off' is a phrase that springs to mind. Having done that, get on with something that is positive and, preferably, enjoyable. The key is to replace negative thoughts with positive ones and/or actions. Instead of using your imagination to trick the guard into thinking there is a danger (worrying), you use it to tell it that "everything's OK". Do this and it will stand down and stop sending out those damned stress hormones.

Remember, in Chapter 3 we learned that when we're emotionally aroused, we become stupid. So if those worries and ruminations get a grip on you before you even realise it (they tend to creep up on us) you can calm yourself down (and regain access to your thinking brain) by doing a simple breathing exercise.

It's called 7/11. Sit down, relax and, if you like, close your eyes. Begin to breathe slowly and evenly, preferably from the diaphragm, and then start to slow down the out-breath by breathing in to a count

73

of seven, and out to a count of eleven.

Do this for five or ten minutes and you'll feel more relaxed and have more brain power, too!

Action Three – Get on your bike!

Get active. Because too much dream sleep makes us feel utterly knackered (all our 'get up and go' has 'got up and gone', remember?) activity is the last thing we feel like when we're depressed. Lying under a duvet on the sofa watching old movies and dreadful afternoon television is about all we can bring ourselves to do. *Big mistake*.

Not only does this make it much less likely that we will be able to get to sleep at night, it reduces our blood chemistry to the state of toxic waste!

Get as active as you can. For some people this may only be going for a gentle walk, for others a jog, a game of squash, a cycle ride, a swim. Preferably something you enjoy. If all else fails, put on some music you enjoy and bop around the house.

Physical activity naturally raises the level of serotonin in the body. It's a feel-good chemical that plays many roles in the mind-body system. One is to help regulate our dream sleep – just what we need when we're in the depressive cycle. Don't push it, don't be silly, do what you can and not what you can't, but *do* something.

Action Four – Have fun!

Get out there and enjoy yourself! If you're in your 80s that may mean getting back into the garden, going to Bingo or down the Legion, or whatever activity you enjoy (or used to enjoy before anxiety or depression sapped your energy). If you're younger, just get back out there with your friends again. Don't let that little voice inside tell you, "You won't enjoy it, you'll just be miserable and spoil everybody's night out." As with worry, tell it to bugger off.

To start with, you might have to act happy even if you are still feeling pretty ghastly. But the more you do this, the more the 'guard' is kept in 'stand-by' mode and will keep the stress hormones under lock and key. Laughter is a really good medicine. It has been clinically shown that laughter, and even the act of physically smiling, releases endorphins – nature's natural morphine – and makes us feel better. So go to the movies to see a good comedy, or down-load some videos; Billy Connolly or Victoria Wood always does it for me – whatever does it for you, *do it.*

Action Five – Stop eating crap!

Stop filling your body with rubbish. Our brain and body system is a delicate balance of chemicals; it needs a constant supply of the right nutrients to function properly. If we eat junk, we won't be giving our body – and that includes our brain – what it needs to work efficiently. Make sure you get plenty of fresh fruit and vegetables, and drink lots of fresh water. You don't have to give up the booze, but remember that alcohol is toxic and puts a real strain on the liver in particular. If you drink like a fish, you'll end up with a brain like one. Don't eat too much red meat (it's difficult to digest); lean white meat is better for you.

Omega 3 oil is especially good for brain function, and is found particularly in oily fish such as salmon and mackerel. If you don't eat much fresh fish, take some Omega 3 supplements.

Try to avoid too much refined sugar and white flour, or products containing them. They just send rushes of glucose into the bloodstream causing, in turn, the release of high levels of insulin, which turns the excess straight into body fat. Remember, you are what you eat, so cut out junk foods!

Most depression and anxiety is easily treated once we know the key. The above five actions when understood *and undertaken* (it doesn't work by osmosis, you have to *do it*), can be enough in themselves to lift depression and anxiety fast.

But what about anti-depressant drugs? They do work for some people, some of the time. The one thing they all have in common is that they reduce the amount of dream sleep we have. It has been shown in sleep laboratories that when people with depression are woken during dream sleep periods, they are less depressed the following day. Less dream sleep equals less exhaustion equals more energy the next day. So far so good.

But all drugs have side effects, and for some people they can be quite nasty. It is also true that while anti-depressants are not addictive inasmuch as people do not crave more and more of them, they can have some very serious withdrawal effects. The drug industry refers to this as 'discontinuation symptoms', a neat expression if you wish to disguise the fact that coming off anti-depressants can make you feel like shit. Unfortunately, discontinuation symptoms can be confused – by both sufferer and doctor – with a return of the original symptoms. So the medication may be reintroduced, with possibly even an increase in dosage.

WARNING!

If you are on anti-depressant medication and you are beginning to feel better, *don't just stop*. Speak with your doctor and agree a slow withdrawal period. It is better to take several weeks, or even months, to come off the medication slowly and appropriately, rather than too quickly and suffer discontinuation symptoms. A very helpful book, useful to both doctors and sufferers alike, is by Joseph Glenmullen (you'll find the details at the back of this book).

Chapter 8

To Conclude

For very many people with anxiety and/or depression, just following the guidelines in this little book will be enough to lift the symptoms and start making life worthwhile again. But what if there is a need for extra help?

If there are real and actual problems in your life that are causing you to get worried, stressed and anxious, then they must be dealt with. To address only the symptoms of stress anxiety and depression, if there are still life events that are causing the problem, will not be much use. It would be a bit like giving a person a walking stick because they have a stone in their shoe. If the problems are beyond your immediate ability to deal with, seek help. Symptoms caused by an active problem will not be cured whilst the active problem remains.

Traditional psychotherapy and counselling tended to look to the past for the cause of our current problems. The assumption was that problems or difficult situations from our personal history have caused us to react badly to things now. There is of course some truth in this. Patterns of thought and behaviour repeated over years can be detrimental to our current health. But, generally speaking, months or years of frequent psychoanalysis or counselling are not necessary. In fact, given the nature of the guard, doing psychological archaeology should be positively discouraged for people with depression.

Thinking about all the awful things that may have happened to us over the years, will simply put the guard into overdrive. As it can't tell the difference between a current threat to our survival, and bad memories from the past, a few hours of psychotherapy can set off a full blown depression even if we weren't depressed before we started.

It is not unusual to hear of people going into counselling or psychotherapy and getting worse rather than better. That is not how it should be.

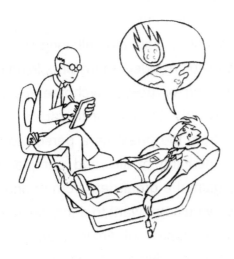

Modern solution-focused therapies – ones that do not rely on archaic dogmatic psychological belief systems - can deal quickly and effectively with most problems. People with traumas, (post-traumatic stress disorder) phobias, anxiety, panic attacks and depression can all respond extremely well to short, solution-focused methods of treatment. Trauma and phobias will often be treatable in just one or two sessions.

We are a free society, and so we are all quite at liberty if we wish to spend thousands of pounds and hundreds of hours having our entire life psycho-analysed. But it's just possible that, if a person is suffering from stress, anxiety or depression, it could do you more harm than good.

This is not to say that all long-term therapy should always be avoided; many people gain a great deal from having on-going psychotherapy sessions. In modern society the secular therapist has largely taken over from the priest as a person to talk with about 'the meaning of life' and our place in it. I personally gained a great deal from a long Jungian analysis, so would not want to decry such methods. But for the treatment of anxiety, depression and its associated conditions, short, solution-focused therapies are usually best as a first port of call.

So, to reclaim your life from chronic stress, anxiety or depression, here's what you should remember.

1. Understand what causes depression.

2. Too many stress hormones equals excessive emotional arousal.

3. Excessive dream sleep is needed to deactivate the arousal.

4. This is a twenty four hour cycle that needs breaking. To break it, you need to:

Change your style of thinking

Stop worrying and ruminating

Get physically active

Start doing enjoyable things again

Eat a balanced diet

The answer to getting better from the symptoms of anxiety or depression is simple – *but not easy.* Understanding that it is caused by a twenty-four hour cycle of excessive stress and emotional arousal is the key to getting better, but we need to take the actions that will make the difference. Just as learning to drive a car is simple, but not (for most of us) easy, doing what we need to do to recover from our anxiety or depression also requires some effort on our part. We need to apply ourselves to the task, and keep practicing.

This book is a brief guide only. You may wish

to explore more deeply some of the areas touched upon here.

Some other useful books

The Antidepressant Solution
Joseph Glenmullen

Human Givens: The New Approach to Emotional Health and Clear Thinking
Ivan Tyrrell and Joe Griffin

Why We Dream
Joe Griffin and Ivan Tyrrell

The 7 Habits of Highly Effective People
Stephen R Covey

Emotional Intelligence
Daniel Goldman

Websites

www.humangivens.com

www.counselling-directory.org.uk

About the author:

Chris Scott has worked as a psychologist, trainer, counsellor, psychotherapist and organisational consultant. For over thirty years he has also been an ordained Anglican priest working in both parishes and chaplaincy. Chris is particularly interested in the interface between religion and psychology; especially those areas which enhance human wellbeing. Married to writer and broadcaster Ruth Scott, they have two grown-up children.

About the illustrator:

Tom Woodbridge spends most of his time making things out of pixels. He has worked as an illustrator, animator, and videogame developer. At the moment he lives and works in Guildford, where he is developing games with the goal of cheering people up.

Lightning Source UK Ltd.
Milton Keynes UK
UKOW05f1856050117
291493UK00017B/632/P

9 781911 076179